The Ground and the Glory:
A Listener's Guide to the Baroque and Folk Continuum in UK Music

by R.H. Mason

The Ground and the Glory: A Listener's Guide to the Baroque and Folk
Continuum in UK Music
by R.H. Mason
ISBN: 978-1-989647-81-3
First published October 12, 2025
Toronto, Ontario

Publisher: The Evergreen Centre

Publisher's Cataloging-in-Publication Data
Mason, R.H.
The Ground and the Glory: A Listener's Guide to the Baroque and Folk
Continuum in UK Music / R.H. Mason. – First edition.

Summary: An academic yet accessible listener's guide that analyzes the
shared structural DNA and ongoing fusion between 17th-century UK
Baroque music (Purcell, Marais) and the 20th-century British Folk Revival
(Fairport Convention, The Copper Family), focusing on core elements like
the ground bass, a cappella performance, and instrumental textures.

Identifiers: ISBN 978-1-989647-81-3

Subjects: Music History. | Folk Music. | Baroque Music. | Music—Great
Britain—History. | Music Criticism. | Music—Analysis, appreciation.

Classification: 781.62—dc23

The Ground and the Glory:
A Listener's Guide to the Baroque and Folk Continuum in UK Music

by R.H. Mason

CHAPTECH SERIES

APPLIED VERNACULAR

A Note on the Series: Applied Vernacular

Welcome to the Chaptech / Applied Vernacular Series.

Chaptech / Applied Vernacular is the art of small, humble books that make knowledge tangible, practical, and joyfully human. Born from the earnest spirit of 1970s scout manuals, National Park pamphlets, mimeographed guides, and the enduring wisdom of the Appropriate Technology Library, this series champions the book as a talisman—a compact, personal artifact designed for engagement, not consumption. We celebrate line drawings that verge on the naïve, the charm of deliberately imperfect diagrams, and the sacred, tactile nature of hand-assembled care. This is instruction as intimacy, expertise as invitation, and the small book as a gateway to doing, making, and discovering.

In a world brimming with fleeting, disembodied information, this collection stands as a quiet testament to enduring knowledge—the kind learned by hand, observed with patience, and proven by practice. Each book is a cultural pocket oratory: an invitation to quiet contemplation and a "first experiment" into a specific facet of the natural world, cultural archives, or practical craft. We celebrate the Applied Vernacular: the language of hands-on wisdom, rooted in everyday experience and the ingenious solutions found in local living. These aren't exhaustive encyclopedias; they are humble field notes, concise guides designed to spark curiosity and equip you with foundational skills and uncommon insights.

This volume, The Ground and the Glory, extends the "field guide" concept to the realm of deep listening, cultural reclamation, and intellectual craft. It treats the arcane connections between Baroque and Folk music as a geological cross-section—a hidden structure waiting to be mapped, understood, and applied. The observations contained within are guides to the ear, inviting you to identify shared patterns, structural DNA (like the ground bass), and the evolution of technique across centuries, making the complexity of music history tangible and usable.

Carry this book with you. Let it be the small weight that anchors your attention, a portable point of reflection. Let it get dog-eared, stained by soil, or marked with your own insights. Use it to deepen your connection to the world around you, to cultivate a quiet competence, and to rediscover the profound satisfaction that comes from knowledge in hand, and practice in heart.

Table of Contents

THE UNIFIED MUSICAL SEED

Introduction
The Lost Lineage: Why This Specific Fusion Matters

This isn't a guide to classical music. This is a guide to time travel.

For too long, the narrative of English musical history has been neatly cleaved in two: on one side, the refined, courtly grandeur of the Baroque era (roughly 1600–1750); on the other, the rough-hewn, enduring spirit of the folk tradition. We've been taught to see these as separate rivers—one flowing through grand concert halls, the other trickling through taverns and fields.

This guide argues they are, in fact, two powerful currents within the same great flow. The Baroque in England wasn't a mere import from Italy or France; it was a native adaptation, infused with the melancholic introspection that echoes the unadorned laments of rural singers centuries earlier. Folk music, meanwhile, wasn't static—it evolved alongside courtly innovations, borrowing rhythmic structures and melodic turns while preserving its oral, communal soul.

The music of the Baroque era in the UK—what we call Baroque UK—was driven by intimate expression, deeply felt emotion, and a fascination with repeating, hypnotic structures. Composers like Henry Purcell crafted works that balanced European sophistication with an English restraint, often evoking the quiet despair of island weather. Meanwhile, the enduring folk tradition preserved the stories, dialects, and simple, profound melodies of the common people—tunes passed from shepherd to plowman, unaltered by notation yet resilient through plagues, wars, and enclosures.

Both sought to express something fundamental about the human condition, often with just a few instruments or an unaccompanied voice. In Purcell's descending bass lines, we hear the same inexorable pull as in a folk dirge's repeated refrain; in a Sussex family's a cappella ballad, the raw vulnerability mirrors the chamber intimacy of a viol consort.

The connection isn't always obvious. You won't find George Frideric Handel here, whose grand, European-style operas often overshadowed the native English composers. Nor will you find the Romantic sweep of Beethoven. Our focus is narrower: the period when English Baroque composers like Henry Purcell were absorbing European styles while retaining a distinctly English melancholy—a "sweetness and light" tempered by Puritan shadows and civil unrest. And how the ancient, living folk music continued—sometimes underground during Cromwell's Interregnum, sometimes resurfacing at Restoration courts—as a powerful, foundational counterpoint.

This fusion matters because it reveals a hidden continuity in English identity. The Baroque's structured repetition wasn't alien to folk ears; it was an amplification of the drone and ostinato already humming in village halls. Folk narratives, with their stark moral arcs, prefigured the dramatic arias of opera. By exploring these threads, we reclaim a musical heritage that's not elitist or rustic, but profoundly human—intimate, historical, and fused.

This is expertise for engagement. Our goal isn't just to listen, but to understand the DNA of this music: the ground bass that structures grief, the unaccompanied voice that carries a hundred-year-old story, and the simple dance rhythm that underpins both courtly suites and village merriment. We'll dissect structures, trace influences, and provide actionable listening prompts to make these pieces your own.

Prepare your ears. We are listening for the shared heartbeat—a pulse that beats from Whitehall to the Weald, from 1689 to today.

Historical Echoes: A Brief Timeline of Fusion

To ground our journey, consider this timeline of key moments where Baroque and folk intertwined:

- **1651:** John Playford publishes *The English Dancing Master*, codifying folk-derived dances for the gentry amid post-Civil War recovery.

- **1670s:** Matthew Locke scores incidental music for Shakespeare's *The Tempest*, blending theatrical ostinatos with popular jig rhythms.

- **1689:** Purcell's *Dido and Aeneas* premieres, its ground bass echoing the lament forms of earlier English ayres.

- **1695:** John Blow mourns Purcell with an ode, using chamber forces that nod to domestic folk gatherings.

- **18th Century:** Turlough O'Carolan, the Irish harper, composes in a Baroque-folk hybrid, influencing UK traditions.

- **20th Century Revival:** Shirley Collins and Nic Jones revive ballads, their arrangements subtly echoing Purcell's melodic contours.

This isn't exhaustive, but it sketches the web we'll explore.

THE GROUND BASS AS A FOUNDATION.

Part I: Foundations – The Baroque Emotional Core
Chapter 1: Grief and the Ground Bass

The Purcell Lament: Henry Purcell - "Dido's Lament"

Few pieces of music capture the weight of sorrow as perfectly as **Henry Purcell's "Dido's Lament"** (from his 1689 opera Dido and Aeneas). Based on Nahum Tate's libretto drawn from Virgil's Aeneid, it depicts Queen Dido's suicidal despair as Aeneas abandons her for Italy. When Dido prepares for death, the musical underpinning is not a static chord or a soaring melody, but a repeating, descending figure called a **ground bass** (or basso ostinato).

Historical Context: Purcell's World

Purcell (1659–1695) was a child of the Restoration, born just after the monarchy's return in 1660. His music bridged the austere Commonwealth era—when music was suppressed—and the exuberant Stuart court. *Dido and Aeneas* was likely composed for a girls' school in Chelsea, blending operatic ambition with educational restraint. The lament's intimacy reflects this: it's a chamber work, not a spectacle, performed with minimal forces like strings and continuo.

Listening Focus: The Ground Bass Structure

A ground bass is a short melodic pattern that is repeated over and over in the lowest voice (the bass line) while the upper voices—in this case, the singer Dido—develop variations and new melodies above it. Purcell uses a **descending chromatic line** (a line that moves stepwise, using all the half-steps, giving it a heavy, dragging quality). It spans a perfect fourth from tonic to dominant, harmonized with poignant suspensions. It sounds inescapable. It is the musical equivalent of a fixed fate. The four-bar phrase repeats fifty times in total, creating a foundation of relentless, controlled grief.

Listening Action: Hearing the Inevitability

Instead of trying to play it, or map it on notation software, let your ear focus only on the lowest sound (the cello and bass instruments).

1. **Isolate the Anchor:** Listen to the very start of the aria. The deep instruments play the ground bass figure alone for a few seconds. Notice how it **descends slowly** and sounds like a sigh or a sinking feeling.

2. **Count the Cycle:** This short bass phrase is four bars long. Once Dido begins singing, try to notice when the bass line repeats. It acts like a **musical metronome of sorrow**, starting over every few seconds.

3. **Hear the Conflict:** Listen to how Dido's highly expressive, soaring melody fights against this simple, repeating pattern. Her voice is desperate, but the bass line is calm, relentless, and final. It tells you the outcome before she finishes her lament.

4. **Connect Sound and Text:** Notice how the emotional repetitions in the text—"Remember me, but ah! forget my fate"—are amplified by the endless repetition in the music's foundation. The text and the bass line are locked in a cycle of grief.

§

Deeper Dive: Cultural Resonance

In 17th-century England, death was omnipresent—plague, fire, war. The lament's structure ritualizes loss, much like folk keening. Scholars like Peter Holman note its influence on later English song, from Dowland to Elgar. Listen to Jessye Norman's 1980s recording for a voice that embodies regal fragility.

Intimate Loss: John Blow - Ode on the Death of Mr. Henry Purcell

When Purcell died prematurely in 1695 at age 36—likely from tuberculosis—his mentor **John Blow** composed an extraordinary *Ode on the Death of Mr. Henry Purcell*. Text by John Dryden, it premiered soon after, a testament to their bond: Blow had taught Purcell at the Chapel Royal.

Historical Context: Mentorship and Mortality

Blow (1649–1708) outlived Purcell but shared his fate as a court composer.

The ode, published in 1696, reflects the era's elegiac fashion, akin to In Nomines for viols. It was scored for intimate forces, underscoring the personal scale of Baroque grief.

Listening Focus: Instrumentation and Personal Intimacy

Unlike the grand orchestras of continental Europe, much of the finest English Baroque was written for smaller, more personal ensembles.

Blow's Ode is a superb example, scored for two countertenors, two recorders (flutes), and *basso continuo*—harpsichord or organ with bass viol. The sound is delicate and mournful, often featuring the **viol** family (*viola da gamba*), which possesses a less assertive, more breathy sound than the modern violin.

- **Action 1:** Isolate the recorders in a recording (e.g., by The King's Consort). Their reedy timbre evokes wind through Westminster Abbey, where Purcell was buried.

- **Action 2:** Note the countertenors' interplay—high, ethereal voices that blend like whispers, contrasting the bass's grounding.

- **Intimacy:** This music was designed for the private chambers of the wealthy, not a massive public arena. The small scale amplifies the feeling of personal loss, making it a musical elegy from one friend and colleague to another. The grief here is less theatrical than Dido's; it is immediate and specific, with Dryden's lines ("The Musick that him serv'd to adore") weaving grief into praise.

§

Deeper Dive: Scholarly Echoes

Musicologist Bruce Wood describes it as "a masterpiece of restrained passion," highlighting its motivic echoes of Purcell's own style.
For a fusion hint, compare to folk elegies like the Copper Family's unaccompanied laments—both honor the dead through simple repetition.

THE VIOLA DA GAMBA CONSORT.

Part 1. Chapter 2: Hypnosis and Variation

The Repeating Line: Matthew Locke - Curtain Tune on a Ground

The fascination with repetition was not limited to expressing grief. It was a core structural element of the Baroque mindset, and it could be used to build immense tension and drama. ***Matthew Locke's Curtain Tune on a Ground*** (from the 1674 adaptation of Shakespeare's The Tempest) exemplifies this.

Historical Context: Theatre and Tempest

Locke (1621–1677), a viol player and composer, scored incidental music for Dryden and Davenant's *The Tempest*. The "Curtain Tune" opens the storm scene, using music to conjure chaos—mirroring the play's themes of control and release.

Listening Focus: The Ostinato–The Relentless Repeating Bass Figure

The term ostinato is often used interchangeably with ground bass, but it emphasizes the *stubbornness* of the repetition. Locke's *Curtain Tune* is a remarkable sonic image of a storm brewing, starting placid before erupting.

- **Action 1:** The music begins with a stark, unsettling, short bass pattern in D minor that is immediately set on repeat. Listen to how the other voices and instruments start to swirl and build tension over this static foundation—violins adding rapid scales like gathering winds.

- **Action 2: Mark the shifts:** From calm (mm. 1-8) to fury (post-variation 4). How does the ostinato remain unmoved amid the upper chaos?

- **Tension:** The upper parts become increasingly complex and agitated, using fast runs and dissonant harmonies, but they never truly break free from the bass line. This relentless, unmoving lower voice grounds the sonic chaos, creating a hypnotic, driving, and almost cinematic tension. It's an early example of using repetition not just for sorrow, but for dramatic, building excitement—prefiguring film scores.

Deeper Dive: Locke's Legacy

Locke championed English polyphony against French imports, his tunes influencing Playford's collections. Hear it in The Brandenburg Consort's recording for authentic viols.

Virtuosic Meditation: Heinrich Biber - Passacaglia for Solo Violin

While **Heinrich Biber** was Bohemian (1644–1704), his **Passacaglia for Solo Violin** (from the Mystery Sonatas, c. 1676) is a masterwork in the Baroque tradition of the repeating bass and provides the ultimate solo meditation on the structure. Dedicated to Marian mysteries, it caps the set as a guardian angel's vigil.

Historical Context: Scordatura and Spirituality

Biber's use of **scordatura** (retuned strings) was innovative, but the Passacaglia is standard-tuned, emphasizing purity. Composed for Salzburg's court, it blends Italian variation with German depth.

- Biber was renowned for his innovative and extensive use of scordatura (Italian for "mistuning"), the practice of intentionally tuning the strings of a string instrument to pitches other than the standard G-D-A-E (for the violin).

- **Technical Innovation:** Scordatura allowed Biber to achieve unusual chord voicings, resonances, and technical effects on the violin that would be impossible or exceedingly difficult in standard tuning. Each unique tuning essentially created a "new" instrument.

- **The Rosary Sonatas:** Biber's most famous set of works employing scordatura is the 'Mystery' or 'Rosary' Sonatas (c. 1676). Each of the fifteen sonatas (corresponding to the fifteen mysteries of the rosary) uses a different scordatura.

- **Spiritual Symbolism:** The varying tunings in the Rosary Sonatas are integral to the programmatic and spiritual content of the music. For instance, the tuning for the Crucifixion sonata (10th sonata) crosses the middle strings, visually and aurally symbolizing the cross.

Biber's compositional style achieves a masterful synthesis of 17th-century European music, blending the brilliant virtuosity, lyrical expression, and variation forms of the Italian Baroque (like those by Corelli) with the contrapuntal complexity, deep spiritual purpose, and meditative forms (such as the Passacaglia) characteristic of the German tradition. This dual approach allowed his music, composed for the cosmopolitan Salzburg court, to be simultaneously technically innovative and profoundly expressive.

Listening Focus: Technical Difficulty and Spiritual Depth

A **Passacaglia** is yet another term for a piece built upon a ground bass, often one that repeats a four-note descending tetrachord (e.g., A-G-F-E). What makes Biber's piece astonishing is that the ground bass is implied — it is *internalized* by a single, unaccompanied violin.

- **Action 1:** The piece begins with the simple, descending four-note theme in the lowest register of the violin. Listen for how the violinist then performs dazzling feats of polyphony (creating the illusion of multiple voices) while constantly ensuring that the repeated bass line is subtly sounded, either explicitly or implied in the lowest note of a chord.

- **Action 2:** Count variations (over 60!): Early ones simple, later fugal. Focus on double-stops for harmonic richness.

- **Depth:** The piece is a demanding test of virtuosity, but its ultimate effect is spiritual. The relentless, simple repetition of the bass line acts as an anchor for the listener's ear, allowing the complex, soaring variations above to feel like a contemplative journey — a musical prayer tethered to a fixed, earthly foundation.

§

Deeper Dive: Cross-Cultural Ties

While Central European composer Heinrich Biber utilized his innovative style across the continent, his monumental Passacaglia achieved cross-cultural recognition by circulating in manuscript as far as England. Its form is structurally similar to English "divisions on a ground," a genre where composers like **John Jenkins** developed virtuosic variations over a repeated bass pattern. These ties highlight the shared musical language of the Baroque era, and modern interpreters like violinist **Rachel Podger** continue to capture the work's profound ecstasy and meditative power for contemporary audiences.

Building on the structural and spiritual parallels, one might speculate that Biber's Passacaglia offered a historic precedent for the **long-form, cyclical bass motif**, a technique later central not only to the unique voice of **Eberhard Weber** but also to the meditative, ground-based compositional framework found in the work of other Nordic Jazz pioneers like **Jan Garbarek** and **Tord Gustavsen**.

THE A CAPPELLA CIRCLE

Part II: The Solo Voice – Timeless Folk Ballads
Chapter 3: The Unaccompanied Truth

Oral Tradition: The Copper Family – Shepherd of the Downs

If the Baroque relied on formal structure, the folk tradition relied on the pure, unadorned voice. The tradition of the **Copper Family** from Sussex is arguably the most famous example of a living, unbroken folk lineage in England. Tracing their tradition to the 1820s, they've sung without instruments (a cappella), preserving agrarian tales.

Historical Context: Rottingdean Roots

The Coppers—including Bob and Ron—were farmers and shepherds on the South Downs in Sussex, a region geographically central to the entire South-East English folk tradition. Their songs are closely tied to ancient customs like May Day rites and harvest celebrations. Recorded in the 1950s by Bob Copper, *Shepherd of the Downs* (also known as *Shepherd in Love*) is one of their oldest tunes, possibly dating to the 18th century.

Key Artists and Recording Periods

The Copper Family's music wasn't "written" in the modern sense but preserved orally and then committed to paper and tape by various family members and collectors, primarily during the mid-20th century.

First Preservation (1898): The songs were first formally collected by Kate Lee, one of the founders of the Folk Song Society, who noted them down from James 'Brasser' Copper (1845–1924) and his brother Thomas Copper (c. 1847–c. 1936). This early collection work was foundational to the First English Folk Revival.

The Revival Generations (1950s–1970s): The family gained widespread recognition during the Second Revival thanks to the singing of Bob Copper (1915–2004) and his cousin Ron Copper (c. 1913–1979). Their voices, captured in the early 1950s, became a touchstone of authenticity.

Initial Recordings (1951): The BBC's recording of Bob and his father, Jim Copper (1882–1954), in 1951, followed by sessions with folklorists like Peter Kennedy throughout the decade, brought their a cappella harmonies into the national consciousness, making them revered figures by the early 1960s.

Important Recordings and Legacy Albums

The Coppers are primarily known for their unadorned performances on a handful of influential releases that served as vital inspiration for the emerging 1960s folk artists:

* **Traditional Songs From Rottingdean (1963):** This album, compiling Peter Kennedy's recordings, was one of their earliest formal releases and clearly showcased their distinctive, unforced two-part harmony.

* **A Song for Every Season (1971):** This monumental release cemented their legacy. Originally issued as a 4-LP box set, it featured Bob and Ron singing alongside the next generation (Bob's daughter, Jill, and son, John), accompanied by Bob's spoken narration providing detailed social context for the songs. This set won the Robert Pitman Literary Prize for the accompanying book, elevating the folk tradition to serious literature.

* **Come Write Me Down (2001):** This Topic Records CD compilation of their early 1950s field recordings provides the best listening experience for their raw, original style, capturing classics like "The Banks of the Sweet Primroses" and "The Shepherd of the Downs".

Listening Focus: Lack of Accompaniment, Regional Dialect, and Generational Lineage

The raw power of the unaccompanied voice —**a cappella**—is is the essence of oral tradition, ensuring nothing distracts from the melody, the story, and the unique sound of the voice itself.

- **Action 1:** Focus on the sound of the voices. They sing in natural, unforced harmony, often with a subtle rhythmic freedom that instrumental accompaniment would restrict. Listen for the distinct regional dialect in the pronunciation—for example, "Downs" as "Daaans"—which ties the song directly to the landscape of the South Downs.

- **Action 2:** Trace the drone-like bass harmony. It holds like a ground bass, letting the tenor lead the lover's plea, thus creating a simple but potent emotional foundation that echoes Baroque chamber odes.

- **Lineage:** This is not a performance for an audience; it's a song for the family and community. The lack of accompaniment makes the listener an intimate guest in a private tradition, allowing the history carried in the collective memory to be felt directly.

Transition to Shirley Collins

It is this specific South Downs heritage and unadorned vocal philosophy that ties the Coppers directly to the next great figure of the revival: Shirley Collins, a younger local artist who inherited and championed the same regional tradition.

§

Shirley Collins: Fragile Timelessness and the Folk Revival

Shirley Collins (b. 1935) is one of the most vital figures of the English folk music revival of the mid-20th century. Her career, spanning recordings from the 1950s–1970s, is characterized by a commitment to authenticity and archaic style, bridging the archival work of the first revival with the raw approach of the second.

Historical Context: Revival and Roots

The English Folk Revival aimed to rediscover and popularize the traditional songs of rural Britain.

- **First Revival (Late 19th/Early 20th Century):** Led by collectors like Cecil Sharp and Ralph Vaughan Williams, this phase preserved songs in print but often sanitized and harmonized them for academic or concert presentation.

- **Second Revival (Mid-20th Century):** This more influential period sought an unadorned, raw performance style, often inspired by the American folk boom. Key figures presented songs using natural ornamentation, modal scales, and the emotional directness found in original field recordings.

Collins's work perfectly encapsulates this second revival's quest for authenticity. Her personal style is a synthesis of:

- **The Appalachian Field Trips (1959):** The critical event of her early career was her seven-month field trip across the American South with musicologist Alan Lomax. This journey exposed her to archaic English ballads preserved in isolated Appalachian communities in forms purer than those surviving back home, informing her vocal techniques.

- **Kentish Roots:** Her singing was equally shaped by her Kentish family, especially her Aunt Dolly and Aunt Grace Wingrave, providing a direct, familial link to the songs and natural, regional singing style of South-East England.

§

Listening Focus: The Ground and the Delivery

The song *"Just as the Tide Was Flowing"* (Roud 1105), a buoyant courtship song that Collins learned fragmentarily and expanded over four recordings, is a prime example of her aesthetic.

- **"Gentle, Almost Ethereal" Voice:** Her delivery is famously unadorned, clear, and direct, sung in a pure register that emphasizes the narrative and modal melody. This vocal purity, lacking vibrato or dramatic theatrics, embodies the quiet simplicity of the ancient tradition. Her philosophy is that the song's story is paramount.

- **Fragile Timelessness:** The melody is cyclical and deceptively simple, creating a gentle, timeless atmosphere. Note how her breath control and pauses evoke the rhythm of sea tides, subtly mirroring the lyric. This "fragile timelessness" is enhanced by the simple production and slight imperfections, making the listening experience feel immediate and historic.

§

Revival Impact and Cross-Genre Ties

Collins's rigorous pursuit of purity established a crucial touchstone for the entire Second English Folk Revival. Her authentic approach, paralleling the living tradition championed by the Copper Family from nearby Sussex, directly inspired the 1960s folk boom and validated the unembellished, local singing style. The Coppers' foundational importance can still be heard on their 2001 Topic Records release, which archives their deep heritage. Interestingly, Collins's vocal philosophy of prioritizing clarity and simple melodic truth over elaborate display finds an unexpected structural parallel with the ayres (or airs) of Baroque composer **Henry Purcell** from the late 17th century; both traditions are united in their demand for unadorned, clear text setting. While deeply traditional, Collins also demonstrated a capacity for subtle fusion, notably with her 1971 recording alongside the **Albion Country Band** on the album *No Roses*. This work, which added subtle instrumentation like fiddle and concertina, served as an essential link to the burgeoning electric folk movement, showing that genuine tradition could embrace modern musical dialogue. Her decades-long commitment to this quest for preservation and history is further chronicled in her 2021 memoir, *All in the Downs*.

THE UNSEEN WEAVE: GUITAR AS CONTINUO.

Part 2. Chapter 4: Narrative and Revival

This chapter explores how the **Second English Folk Revival (c. 1950s–1970s)** took the ancient oral tradition—preserved by source singers like the Copper Family—and transformed it. We trace the movement from the purity of the unadorned voice to the development of virtuosic instrumental arrangement and genre fusion, demonstrating how artists adapted the ballad narrative for the modern age, often drawing thematic and structural inspiration from Baroque forms.

The Master Arranger: Nic Jones - Canadee-I-O

The folk tradition is fundamentally a storytelling tradition, and Nic Jones (b. 1947), a folk revivalist of the 1970s, was a master of arranging these ancient ballads, transforming them through a unique and highly influential guitar style.

Historical Context: Penguin Eggs Era

Jones's 1980 album, *Penguin Eggs*, became a landmark of the revival. It was the culmination of his technical development, featuring complex fingerstyle guitar that treated the folk song structure not as a fragile document, but as a framework for instrumental virtuosity. His brief career was tragically cut short by a car accident in 1982, yet his innovative style permanently influenced guitarists across the genre, including Martin Simpson.

Key Artists and Recording Periods

Jones was active in the folk club scene of the late 1960s, but his most important work was recorded in the 1970s.

- **Early Albums (1970s):** Recordings like Ballads and Songs (1970) and From the Devil and the Deep Blue Sea (1972) established his distinct, rhythmically driving solo acoustic approach.

- **The Signature Album (1980):** Penguin Eggs, featuring "Canadee-I-O" and "The Humpback Whale," solidified his reputation for reinterpreting long-form narratives using advanced guitar techniques.

Important Recordings and Legacy Albums

Jones's solo style demonstrated that complex instrumental arrangement could serve, rather than distract from, the narrative power of the traditional song.

- **Ballads and Songs (1970):** Features his early, driving version of "Canadee-I-O" (Child Ballad 209), a tale of a servant girl's transatlantic elopement.

- **Penguin Eggs (1980):** His definitive work, known for its pristine recording quality and the dense, rhythmic texture of the guitar.

Listening Focus: Analysis of the Narrative Ballad Structure and Jones's Influential Guitar Style

The melody of "Canadee-I-O" remains largely the same throughout, but the story moves forward through dramatic, sequential detail—from the merchant's ship to the queen's court. The music's purpose is to serve the narrative structure, not to develop a theme in the Baroque sense.

- **Action 1: Tune to Open C (CGCGCD):** Jones's innovative use of open tunings and a distinctive, percussive hammer-on and pull-off technique (often called the 'doodle' style) gives his accompaniment a driving, almost mechanized rhythm. This provides the ancient melody with a modern, propulsive energy.

- **Action 2: The Guitar as Continuo:** Note how the accompaniment isn't mere decoration; it acts as a second voice in the narrative, maintaining rhythmic tension and emotional context, much like a Baroque continuo provides a necessary foundation for the vocalist.

§

The Virtuoso Dialogue: Carthy & Swarbrick - The Broomfield Hill

The duo of Martin Carthy (guitar/vocals, b. 1940) and Dave Swarbrick (fiddle, 1941–2020) was critical to the UK folk revival, forming a partnership that created dense, complex arrangements of traditional material using instrumental prowess.

Historical Context: Fairport and Beyond

Carthy and Swarbrick met in the vibrant 1960s folk club scene and quickly established themselves as the preeminent pairing for ins¹trumental folk interpretation.

- **The Bridge to Electric Folk:** Their collaboration was foundational to the formation of Fairport Convention (Carthy joined in 1968), where they directly applied their rigorous arrangement style to the electric format, essentially inventing electric folk.

- **Source Material:** Their material, such as "The Broomfield Hill" (Child Ballad 43), often reflects ancient medieval motifs, in this case, a supernatural wager tale about a test of chastity.

Key Artists and Recording Periods

The careers of Carthy and Swarbrick are tightly intertwined, marking a progression from pure folk arrangement to folk-rock.

- **Early Duets (1965–1968):** Their debut album, Martin Carthy & Dave Swarbrick (1965), featured The Broomfield Hill and established their intricate acoustic arrangement style.

- **Mid-Career (1969–1979):** The pair worked extensively together through Fairport Convention and later in collaborations, continuing to record and evolve their dialogue-based instrumental style.

Important Recordings and Legacy Albums

Their work demonstrated that the traditional ballad could sustain complex, virtuosic arrangement without losing its essential narrative core.

- **Martin Carthy & Dave Swarbrick (1965):** A seminal acoustic album showcasing the revolutionary interplay between fiddle and guitar.

- **But Two Came By (1968):** Further solidified their reputation for tackling challenging ballads with sophistication and energy.

Listening Focus: Discussion of the Guitar/Fiddle Interplay and Narrative Tension

The music here mirrors the dramatic conflict inherent in the ballad's story.

- **Action 1:** Listen to the Conversation: Listen carefully to the conversation between Carthy's rhythmic, angular guitar work (providing the structural tension) and Swarbrick's virtuosic fiddle (weaving around the melody, sometimes in harmony, sometimes providing dissonant commentary). The interplay is tight and complex.

- **Action 2:** Track the Modal Shifts: Note how the music shifts from Mixolydian calm into tense minor keys during the "sleep" verses where the magical test occurs.

- **Tension and Dialogue:** The instruments are locked in a sophisticated dialogue—a rhythmic engine that drives the story forward. Where Baroque music uses repetition for controlled emotion (the ground bass), this folk arrangement uses intricate instrumental interplay to build narrative tension and dramatic propulsion, suggesting a kind of intellectual fusion long before overt genre blending.

§

The Psychological Interpreter: June Tabor - Airs and Graces

June Tabor (b. 1947) represents the revival's shift toward psychological intensity in narrative. Her voice is stark, unadorned (like Collins, but with greater dramatic weight), and utterly focused on extracting the deepest emotional truth from the ballads, often using minimal arrangement.

Historical Context: Austerity and Emotion

Tabor emerged in the 1970s, quickly establishing herself as a distinct voice that prioritized emotional rigor over the emerging instrumental flash. Her approach was often praised for its "austerity," using a controlled delivery to convey profound sorrow or defiance. She proved that the traditional ballad, even without elaborate guitar work, remained the most powerful vehicle for complex human stories.

Key Artists and Recording Periods

Tabor's career has been defined by solo work and lasting, epic collaborations (such as with Maddy Prior in Silly Sisters).

- **Debut Era (1976):** Her first solo album, Airs and Graces (1976), immediately announced her arrival as a major interpreter.

- **Collaboration & Consistence (1980s–Present):** She maintained her reputation for tackling challenging traditional and contemporary folk songs with a consistent focus on vocal precision and narrative clarity.

Important Recordings and Legacy Albums

Tabor's albums are noted for their solemnity and depth, treating each song as a profound dramatic monologue.

- **Airs and Graces (1976):** Features her haunting interpretation of "Pull Down Lads," setting the standard for the serious, unromantic treatment of historical narratives.

- **"And the Band Played Waltzing Matilda":** While a contemporary song, her definitive recording treats the narrative of the wounded veteran with the same gravity as an ancient ballad of war or loss.

Listening Focus: Emotional Precision and Unaccompanied Power

Tabor's style strips away ornamentation, placing all the weight of the story on her vocal performance.

- **Action 1: Focus on Diction and Tempo:** Listen to her precise diction and deliberate pacing. Unlike the speed of Carthy's arrangements, Tabor often slows the songs down, allowing every word of the narrative—particularly lines describing cruelty or consequence—to land with maximum emotional impact.

- **Action 2: Thematic Contrast:** Note how the austerity of her voice sharpens the contrast when she tackles a narrative of profound romance or tragedy, making her restraint an effective tool for dramatic buildup. Her method echoes the formal emotional restraint found in the dramatic monologues of Baroque opera.

§

The Electric Narrator: Steeleye Span - All Around My Hat

Steeleye Span (formed 1969) took the ballads rescued by the revivalists and gave them theatrical spectacle, pioneering the most commercially successful phase of electric folk and proving the dramatic longevity of traditional songs.

Historical Context: Amplifying the Narrative

Formed by key figures including Tim Hart, Maddy Prior, and Ashley Hutchings, Steeleye Span took the detailed traditional narratives (often long, dark Child Ballads) and arranged them for a full electric band (guitar, bass, drums, fiddle). This wasn't fusion for fusion's sake, but a method to provide the epic sweep and thunderous impact necessary for medieval tales of magic, betrayal, and war.

Key Artists and Recording Periods

The band went through various line-ups, but the chemistry between Maddy Prior's sharp, clear vocals and the electric arrangements defined their sound.

- **Early Experimentation (1970–1972):** Albums like Hark! The Village Wait and Below the Salt established their ability to electrify traditional source material.

- **Commercial Peak (1974–1975):** Albums like Now We Are Six and Commoners Crown saw the band achieve mainstream success by injecting rock energy into the traditional repertoire.

Important Recordings and Legacy Albums

Steeleye Span showed how the narrative of the revival could cross over into mainstream pop culture.

- **"Gaudete":** A 1972 a cappella Christmas track that became an unlikely UK chart hit, demonstrating the raw power of collective voices and modal harmony.

- **All Around My Hat (1975):** The title track, a lively version of a traditional song, became their biggest hit, successfully packaging a traditional folk narrative for radio play.

Listening Focus: Narrative Propulsion and Electric Texture

Steeleye Span treated the five-minute traditional ballad like a rock epic.

- **Action 1: Analyze the Rhythmic Engine:** Listen to the use of the bass and drums. They provide a driving, rock rhythm that pushes the ancient melodies forward with urgency, directly contrasting the intimate, unforced rhythm of the Copper Family source recordings.

- **Action 2: The Vocal/Instrumental Power:** Note how Maddy Prior's strong, clear voice cuts through the dense electric texture. She delivers the narrative with a crisp clarity that ensures the story is never lost to the volume, maintaining the folk tradition's core commitment to the text despite the amplification.

§

The Guitar Virtuoso: Bert Jansch - Needle of Death

Bert Jansch (1943–2011) was one of the most significant and influential acoustic guitarists of the 1960s British folk revival. He took the traditional ballad structure and infused it with Baroque, jazz, and blues complexity, treating the acoustic guitar not merely as accompaniment, but as a chamber instrument capable of intricate, contrapuntal melody and rhythm.

Historical Context: Folk-Baroque Fusion

Jansch rose to prominence in the mid-1960s, a period when the folk scene was heavily influenced by American blues and the experimentalism of the counter-culture. His playing style, characterized by sophisticated fingerpicking and complex rhythms, was highly influential, impacting major figures like Jimmy Page (Led Zeppelin) and Paul Simon. He was a founding member of the folk-jazz fusion group Pentangle in 1967, further expanding the boundaries of the genre.

Key Artists and Recording Periods

Jansch's most influential period was his early solo career before the formation of Pentangle.

- **Solo Debut (1965):** His self-titled debut, Bert Jansch (1965), was recorded simply on a reel-to-reel tape machine and immediately set a new standard for acoustic guitar playing.

- The Pentangle Era (1968–1973): As part of Pentangle, he helped create a sophisticated blend of traditional British folk, jazz, and blues, featuring virtuosic group arrangements.

Important Recordings and Legacy Albums

Jansch's albums introduced a level of instrumental artistry that made the traditional song instantly contemporary.

- **Bert Jansch (1965):** Features the powerful narrative protest song "Needle of Death," a stark, unflinching look at drug abuse, delivered over complex, modal fingerpicking.

- **Jack Orion (1966):** An album focused on traditional Child Ballads, notably featuring collaboration with John Renbourn, where they treated long narratives with densely arranged, often unsettling, guitar duets.

Listening Focus: Contrapuntal Guitar and Lyrical Clarity

Jansch's technique is a masterclass in using instrumental complexity to heighten narrative tension.

- **Action 1: Analyze the Fingerstyle:** Listen to how the bass lines, chords, and melody are played simultaneously, often giving the impression of two guitars. This contrapuntal style, drawing inspiration from classical guitar and early music, provides a rich, multi-layered foundation for the simple folk melody.

- **Action 2: The Narrative Edge:** In songs like "Needle of Death," the precise, modal quality of the guitar playing provides a cold, almost detached mood that sharply contrasts with the grim emotional narrative, intensifying the story's impact. The guitar's complexity becomes a substitute for the emotional weight that June Tabor would achieve with pure vocal intensity.

§

The Lutenist's Legacy: John Renbourn - The Cruel Sister

John Renbourn (1944–2015) was the most academically inclined of the 1960s British folk guitarists. While his style was rooted in folk and blues (like Jansch's), he drew heavily from pre-Baroque and Baroque lute music to create complex, elegant arrangements that emphasized clarity, structure, and a chamber-music sensibility.

Historical Context: Classical and Folk Counterpoint

Renbourn's career, primarily as Jansch's duo partner and a co-founder of Pentangle (1967), was defined by sophisticated musical curiosity. He essentially translated the contrapuntal texture of composers like Dowland and Bach onto the steel-string acoustic guitar, proving that traditional ballads could support arrangements as intellectually rigorous as any classical piece.

Key Artists and Recording Periods

Renbourn was a consistent collaborator whose work matured throughout the 1960s and 1970s.

- **Duo Work (1966):** The album Bert and John (1966) showcased his tight interplay with Jansch, balancing Jansch's intensity with his own measured precision.

- **The Pentangle Peak (1968–1973):** His work with the band, featuring intricate arrangements of traditional songs, brought his classical-informed style to a wide audience.

Important Recordings and Legacy Albums

Renbourn's recordings are essential for understanding the structural depth achieved by the acoustic revival.

- **Sir John Alot of Merrie Englandes Musyk Thynge and ye Grene Knyght (1968):** A definitive statement, blending his signature arrangements of Child Ballads with genuine early music pieces, explicitly linking the folk tradition to the Renaissance and Baroque past.

- **"The Cruel Sister":** Pentangle's epic version of this ballad is a showcase of Renbourn's measured, precise playing, which forms a dense, interwoven texture with the sitar-like rhythms of Jansch, creating a compelling, multi-layered narrative accompaniment.

Listening Focus: Baroque Structure and Elegance

Renbourn's playing style is the direct aesthetic analogue to the Baroque formality discussed earlier in the chapbook.

- **Action 1:** Analyze the Textures: Listen for the clarity of his independent melodic lines. Unlike the percussive attack of Nic

Jones, Renbourn prioritizes elegance, space, and polyphony—his guitar work sounds almost like a Baroque suite being played as an accompaniment.

- **Action 2:** The Lute Connection: His choice of material and melodic ornamentation often directly reflects the style of the 17th-century English lutenists. This intellectual rigor elevated the traditional ballad, demonstrating that its narrative power was strong enough to survive sophisticated, cross-genre arrangement.

§

The Ensemble: Pentangle - Virtuosity and Fusion

Pentangle (1967–1973), co-founded by guitarists Bert Jansch and John Renbourn, along with vocalist Jacqui McShee, bassist Danny Thompson, and drummer Terry Cox, represents the ultimate realization of acoustic folk fusion.

Historical Context: The Chamber Folk Quintet

Pentangle moved far beyond the simple arrangement of the folk club scene, applying the disciplines of jazz, blues, and early music to the traditional British repertoire. Their sound was a virtuosic, highly complex form of "chamber folk," characterized by dazzling, interwoven instrumental textures.

Key Artists and Contribution

The band's genius lay in the complexity of its rhythm section and the unique blend of its guitarists.

- Jacqui McShee provided a clear, jazz-inflected vocal delivery that was narrative but sophisticated, contrasting with the earthier style of singers like Collins or Prior.

- Thompson and Cox introduced complex, fluid jazz rhythms, allowing the narrative folk tunes to be played with a speed and syncopation previously unknown in the genre.

Important Recordings and Legacy Albums

Pentangle achieved critical acclaim and commercial success by treating the ballad as a launchpad for extended, improvisatory musical exploration.

- **Basket of Light (1969):** Their most successful album, featuring the hit single "Light Flight."

- **Cruel Sister (1970):** Contains their definitive, epic 20-minute rendition of the traditional "Jack Orion", a masterclass in ensemble narrative and instrumental virtuosity.

§

The Psych-Folk Extreme: Forest - The Medieval Trip

Forest (1969–1973) exemplifies the late-revival branch of psychedelic folk (or "acid folk"). While structurally rooted in the traditional ballads, their sound introduced layered, atmospheric arrangements, odd instrumentation, and surreal lyrics, creating a sense of ancient mystery amplified by the counter-culture.

Historical Context: Progressive Minimalism

Formed by the three brothers Martin, Dez, and Hadrian Theobald, Forest utilized a minimal instrumental setup (often just acoustic guitars, cello, and simple percussion) but applied layers of studio effects and vocal harmonies that lent their narratives an ethereal, almost chilling quality.

Key Contribution

Forest's work demonstrated that the narrative heart of folk could be transported into a highly progressive, non-commercial sphere, bridging the gap between traditional tales and the avant-garde.

Forest's Unique and Disturbing Harmonies

The harmonies employed by the three Theobald brothers are crucial to Forest's progressive minimalism, creating an atmosphere that is at once gentle and unsettling. Unlike the communal, hearty harmonies of the Copper Family or the clear, controlled vocal lines of June Tabor, Forest's vocals function almost as a choral texture to support a surreal narrative.

Modal and Tonal Ambiguity

Forest frequently utilizes vocal arrangements built on modal scales (especially those with flattened 7ths, common in folk) rather than strict major or minor keys. This creates a sense of tonal ambiguity, which is inherently unsettling to ears accustomed to Western diatonic harmony.

- **Open Intervals:** Their harmonies often emphasize open intervals (fourths and fifths) and cluster voicings that are close together, avoiding the comfortable resolution of typical folk or rock harmonies. This leaves the sound feeling suspended and unresolved, enhancing the "eerie" or "chilling" quality.

- **Chanting and Drone:** At times, their vocals regress to a form of chanting or a sustained drone. This technique strips the harmony of forward movement, emphasizing the texture over the melody, drawing listeners into a hypnotic state that feels ritualistic and remote, aligning with the "medieval trip" aesthetic.

Ethereal and Layered Production

Forest made deliberate use of studio techniques to make their voices sound disembodied, enhancing the psychological aspect of their narratives.

- **Layering and Phasing:** The brothers recorded multiple vocal tracks, often layering them slightly out of phase or with heavy reverb and echo. This creates an ethereal, wash-like quality where individual voices blend into an atmospheric soundscape. The lack of distinct individual voices makes the music feel non-human or otherworldly.

- **Vocal Delivery:** The delivery itself is often soft, whispered, or breathy, avoiding the robust projection of mainstream folk singers. This intimacy, combined with the strange acoustic space created by the production effects, gives the listener the disturbing impression of hearing voices from a distance, perhaps from beyond a veil or from deep within a dream.

Narrative Effect: The Surreal and the Archaic

The ultimate effect of these unique harmonies is to support a narrative style that is less about storytelling and more about mood and atmosphere.

- **Ancient Mystery:** By avoiding standard harmonic resolution, the vocals successfully evoke a sound that feels genuinely ancient—more akin to Early Music, madrigals, or plainsong than to contemporary folk.

- **Psychological Edge:** The harmonic instability and ethereal production effectively bridge the gap between traditional folk themes (magic, myth) and the psychedelic counter-culture, making the music sound like a journey through a shared, yet slightly disturbing, medieval hallucination. The harmonies are the primary tool used to transport the listener out of the folk club and into the uncanny realm of the psych-folk extreme.

Important Recordings

Their two albums are prized by collectors for their unique sound.

- **Forest (1969):** Their debut featured acoustic purity layered with atmospheric vocal effects.

- **Full Circle (1970):** Further explored complex harmonies and compositions, with songs that felt less like traditional ballads and more like original medieval dreamscapes.

§

The Extreme Edge: Comus - First Utterance

Comus (active c. 1969–1972) represents the furthest, darkest reach of the psychedelic folk movement. Their single album, *First Utterance* (1971), is a unique, unsettling blend of traditional instruments (acoustic guitar, violin, flute, cello) and deeply disturbing narratives focused on mythology, madness, and violence.

Historical Context: Narrative Horror

While Steeleye Span made the medieval epic theatrical, Comus made it horrifyingly visceral. Their music is characterized by jarring dissonance, chanting, and a frenetic intensity, pushing the narrative of the traditional ballad—which often includes themes of murder, incest, and betrayal—into the realm of avant-garde horror. This extremism provides the final, most unsettling counterpoint to the polite arrangements of the mainstream folk revival.

Key Contribution

Comus's sound is defined by the eerie, high-pitched vocals of Roger Wootton and the dissonant sawing of the violin, creating a texture that feels primal, ritualistic, and far removed from the cozy folk club.

Important Recording

- **First Utterance (1971):** Now a cult classic, known for tracks like "Diana" and "The Herald," which use acoustic instruments to evoke a sense of violent psychological breakdown.

§

The Apex of Fusion: Fairport Convention - Liege & Lief

Fairport Convention (formed 1967) achieved the ultimate synthesis of the folk revival's narratives with rock instrumentation. Their 1969 album, *Liege & Lief*, is universally considered the moment electric folk formally arrived, acting as the commercial and artistic high-water mark that tempered the scene's excesses.

Historical Context: The Full Transformation

The band's final, pivotal shift from a folk-rock group to a purely English folk band was catalyzed by the recruitment of traditional authority Martin Carthy and virtuoso fiddler Dave Swarbrick. Their arrival provided the deep knowledge of source material and the intricate arrangement philosophy that propelled the band's vision, applying the complex structures they developed as a duo to a powerful electric lineup.

Key Contribution

Liege & Lief applied powerful rock rhythms (driven by drummer Dave Mattacks and bassist Ashley Hutchings) to lengthy, complex traditional ballads, resulting in a sound that was both commercial and deeply respectful of the archaic source. Sandy Denny's crystalline, emotionally resonant vocals delivered the narratives with perfect clarity, serving as the powerful, feminine voice of the newly electrified tradition.

Important Recordings and Legacy Albums

Fairport Convention successfully packaged the narrative ballad for a mass audience without compromising the material's integrity.

- **Unhalfbricking (1969):** The album that began the electric folk transition, notably featuring the English ballad "A Sailor's Life," a track running over 11 minutes that heavily featured Swarbrick's expressive fiddle.

THE ELECTRIC FOLK FUSION.

- **Liege & Lief (1969):** The definitive electric folk statement, featuring epic tracks like "Tam Lin" and "Matty Groves," treating the dark themes of the **Child Ballads** with dramatic intensity and orchestral scope.

Listening Focus: Narrative Scale and Orchestration

Fairport demonstrated the potential for the narrative ballad to function on a grand, orchestral scale, offering a polished conclusion to the decade of revivalist experimentation.

- **Action 1: The "Jigsaw" Arrangement:** Listen to the intricate, interlocking instrumental complexity, specifically the constant counterpoint between Swarbrick's fiddle and the acoustic/electric guitars. This method of arrangement, rooted in Carthy's style, is a tight form of ensemble counterpoint designed to maintain narrative drive.

- **Action 2: The Epic Scope:** Note how the addition of Mattacks' powerful, subtle drumming and Hutchings' driving bass lines transforms the narrative's pace, giving stories of supernatural encounters and medieval battles the urgency and drama of a modern cinematic score.

§

The Source (Recap): The Copper Family and the Enduring Song

All the preceding arrangements—from Nic Jones's rhythmic complexity to the orchestral sweep of Pentangle and the dissonance of Comus—ultimately stem from the simple, unadorned songs preserved by families like the Copper Family.

The Copper tradition provides the pure, a cappella benchmark, and serves as the cultural bridge linking the rural past to the Baroque era's chamber forms:

The Ground Bass Echo: Shared Foundations of Narrative

The most compelling structural link lies in the foundation of the music. The natural, drone-like bass harmony consistently sung by Bob and Ron Copper in songs such as *"Shepherd of the Downs"* directly echoes a foundational, organizing concept of Baroque composition: the ground bass (or basso ostinato). This simple, repeating figure is essential to the lament and narrative forms found in works like Purcell's *Dido and Aeneas* (1689). The repetitive nature of the ground bass provides an unwavering musical anchor—a constant against which the melody and narrative can unfold and change. Whether heard in a Sussex field song or a court opera, this shared reliance on a simple, repeating musical foundation allowed both high art and folk art to support and structure complex emotional or lengthy narrative arcs. The rhythmic consistency of the drone, whether played by a viol or sung by a bass voice, provides the emotional and structural stability necessary for powerful storytelling.

Chamber Economy: Focus on the Essential Resources

Furthermore, the raw, compelling power of the Copper Family's collective, unadorned voices—singing entirely a cappella—reflects the chamber economy praised in the odes of composers like John Blow and Henry Purcell. This is a philosophy that prioritizes clarity and narrative force over instrumental excess. The Copper family proves that profound emotional effect and narrative power do not require large forces or elaborate scoring, relying instead on the perfect tuning and timing of human voices. In this way, the Copper tradition validates the Baroque ideal of using only essential, focused resources, where the music serves to illuminate the text. The power of a story, whether sung in the intimate setting of a Rottingdean pub or presented within a private 17th-century court, is found in the direct fidelity to the text and the unforced purity of the performance. The simplicity of the source, ironically, gives it an intellectual sophistication that endures through centuries.

THE VIOLA DA GAMBA SOLOIST

Part III: Dance, Fusion, and Celebration
Chapter 5: Baroque Exuberance and The Viola da Gamba

Courtly Variations: Marin Marais - *Les Folies d'Espagne*

The Baroque period, for all its solemnity, was also an era of elaborate dance and spectacular musical ornamentation. Marin Marais (1656–1728), a French contemporary deeply influential in the UK, created a monumental piece based on a simple, repeating folk melody: *Les Folies d'Espagne* (1701, Book 2 for viola da gamba).

Historical Context: Marais and the Gambists

Trained under Sainte-Colombe, Marais was Louis XIV's gambist. *Les Folies* (on the La Folia chord progression) traveled to England, inspiring Handel and Purcell acolytes.

Listening Focus: The Viola da Gamba's Texture and the Transformation of a Folk Melody

The viola da gamba (a six or seven-stringed instrument) is the quintessential Baroque instrument of intimacy. Its fretted neck and flat bridge give it a delicate, often slightly reedy texture—sympathetic strings adding shimmer.

- **Action 1:** The piece is a set of 32 virtuosic variations on the melody known as La Folia, which originated as a lively, simple Portuguese/Spanish folk tune c. 1490. Listen to how Marais takes this simple, repeating theme (i-VI-VII-III-VII-III-VI-V) and subjects it to breathtaking transformations—from tender to furious.

- **Action 2:** Focus on bow techniques: Sul ponticello for sparkle, harmonics for airiness.

- **Transformation:** The focus is on ornamentation and the sheer ingenuity of the composer. The simple, earthy folk melody is taken to the court and dressed in the most elaborate, shimmering musical lace. It reveals that the core musical ideas—simple, repeating motifs—were the same for folk and court; the difference was in the application and ornamentation.

§

Deeper Dive: Folia's Journey

Jordi Savall's *Hespèrion XXI* recording (2005) links Iberian roots to UK adoption. It's a bridge to Playford's tunes.

Early Dance: Playford's The English Dancing Master
For most people, music was inseparable from movement. John Playford's *The English Dancing Master* (first published 1651) is not a single piece of music but a collection that codified the vast wealth of simple, functional dance tunes popular among the common people—over 100 in the first edition.

Historical Context: Post-Civil War Codification

Playford, a bookseller, captured morris and country dances amid Royalist nostalgia. Tunes like *"The Black Nag"* (a hornpipe) or *"Goddesses"* (an almain) blended folk vitality with court polish.

Listening Focus: The Simple, Functional Rhythm and Instrumentation for Communal Dance

These pieces—tunes like *"The Black Nag"* or *"Goddesses"*—are the polar opposite of Marais's elaborate solo work. They were purely functional.

- **Action 1:** Listen to the straightforward, predictable rhythms. The structure is simple: AABB, often short and easily repeated. This music is designed for predictable, communal movement in a circle, line, or square.

- **Action 2:** Imagine the steps: For *"The Black Nag,"* a gallop in 6/8 time—fiddle leading, tabor drumming.

- **Functionality:** The instrumentation is typically simple: pipe and tabor, or a violin/fiddle and a plucked instrument like cittern. The music is clear, energetic, and unpretentious—major keys, dotted rhythms for bounce. It represents the raw, communal need for music as social glue—a form of simple, enduring folk expression that continued throughout the Baroque period and provides the foundational rhythmic DNA for all the music in this guide.

§

Deeper Dive: Modern Revivals and The Dance Continuum

The enduring rhythmic DNA of Playford's collection ensures that these tunes didn't just stay in history books; they directly fueled modern musical traditions.

Historical Purity and Period Performance

Ensembles dedicated to Early Music, such as Gotham Early Music in the US or The Broadside Band in the UK, continue to record Playford's pieces. Their approach is to reconstruct the music using period instruments (recorders, lutes, early violins) and historical techniques. Listening to these sets highlights the original, unpretentious clarity of the music and offers insight into the soundscape of the 17th-century common hall. This purity of sound validates the simple, functional structure that Marais and other court composers chose to elaborate upon.

Folk Fusion and the Ceilidh Connection

Crucially, the simple, repeating rhythmic structures of tunes like "*The Black Nag*" were never abandoned by the people. They became the building blocks for modern folk dancing, or ceilidhs. Contemporary folk bands draw directly from Playford to create energetic dance sets, often incorporating the very drone and rhythmic propulsion discussed in the Blowzabella section. Blowzabella's own use of the hurdy-gurdy and bagpipes creates a relentless, modern version of the rhythmic energy codified by Playford, making the music both historical and intensely physical. The drone, whether from an early violin or a modern hurdy-gurdy, ensures the dance never loses its constant, earthy foundation.

THE CELTIC HARPER.

Chapter 6: Fusion and Folk Fire

Pipes and Power: Blowzabella – The Rose of Raby

The folk revival of the late 20th century explicitly sought to bridge the gap between ancient traditions and modern instrumentation, culminating in energetic fusion groups. Blowzabella, formed in 1975, is a prime example of harnessing the raw, loud power of continental folk instruments—hurdy-gurdy, bagpipes, and shawms.

Historical Context: A Consort Reborn

Inspired by medieval wind bands, Blowzabella revived drones for festivals. The Rose of Raby (from 2009's The Arts of the Battlefield), tied to the Wars of the Roses, amplifies a simple air with fusion fire.

Listening Focus: Modern Folk Revival Instruments–Hurdy-Gurdy/Bagpipes–and High Energy

The Rose of Raby is an example of a simple tune amplified by an engine of complex sound.

- **Action 1:** Listen for the drone—the continuous low note provided by the hurdy-gurdy and/or the bagpipes. This constant, unmoving sonic foundation is a direct spiritual descendant of the Baroque ground bass or ostinato. It is the sound of the earth, constant and unchanging.

- **Action 2:** Note the shawm's bite over hurdy-gurdy wheel—rhythmic cranks like Locke's ostinato.

- **Energy:** Unlike the contemplative Baroque ground, this drone is used to create immense, driving energy. The melody is high and bright, soaring over the relentless, churning rhythm provided by the hurdy-gurdy's cranked wheel and percussion. This sound is a celebration of the raw, physical joy found in dance music.

Deeper Dive: Battlefield Echoes

Their 2021 release ties to historical reenactments. Compare the drone to Biber's implied bass for fusion depth.

The Meeting Point: The Chieftains - O'Carolan's Concerto

The most famous natural fusion of the two styles lies in the music of Turlough O'Carolan (1670–1738), the blind Irish harper. Patronized by Anglo-Irish gentry, he blended native airs with Corelli's concertos. The contemporary arrangement by The Chieftains (formed 1962) highlights this blend.

Historical Context: Harper's Hybrid

O'Carolan, measles-blinded at 18, composed over 200 airs, touring like a Baroque virtuoso. O'Carolan's Concerto (c. 1720) mimics Italian forms; Carolan's Dream is introspective.

Listening Focus: The Irish Harper's Role in Blending Baroque Style with Native Irish Melody

O'Carolan's work sits perfectly at the intersection: it has the ornamentation, clear sections, and structured movements of the Baroque concerto or sonata, but the melodies are purely native Irish, intended to be played on the harp.

- **Action 1:** Listen to The Chieftains' full-ensemble arrangement of O'Carolan's Concerto. You can clearly hear the structured development and formal balance of the Baroque, yet the instruments — flute, fiddle, uilleann pipes, and traditional harp — give it an unmistakable, ancient Irish timbre.

- **Action 2:** Contrast with a solo harp Carolan's Dream. Here, the ornamentation remains, but the intimacy evokes Blow's ode.

- **Blend:** O'Carolan demonstrated that Baroque structure could be applied to folk melody, proving the two traditions were always compatible, sharing a common language of emotional expression.

Deeper Dive: Chieftains' Legacy
Their medleys (e.g., 1987 Celtic Wedding) popularized O'Carolan globally, influencing UK fusions like Blowzabella.

§

The Celtic Mystic: Van Morrison - Astral Weeks

Van Morrison (b. 1945), the Northern Irish singer, utilized the simple melodic and modal structures of his Celtic heritage but layered them with the instrumental improvisation of jazz and the delicate string textures of Baroque chamber music. This fusion resulted in deeply spiritual and narrative music, bridging the folk past with the modern counter-culture.

Historical Context: Narrative Improvisation

Morrison's 1968 album, Astral Weeks, is the definitive example of this fusion. Recorded primarily with jazz session musicians, the album uses sparse instrumentation—upright bass, acoustic guitar, flute, and strings— to create long, flowing song-poems that feel both improvised and ancient. The music avoids standard pop structure, instead following the narrative and emotional contours of the lyrics, much like the recitative and arias of Baroque opera.

Key Contribution

Morrison's genius lies in using the emotional directness and modal qualities of the Irish folk tradition (a language shared by O'Carolan) and placing it into a rich, fluid arrangement that gives the narrative a mythological scope.

Listening Focus: Jazz Strings and Celtic Mode

- **Action 1:** Follow the narrative flow in the title track, "Astral Weeks." Note how the narrative is sustained not by a repeating chorus, but by the continuous, weaving interplay of the acoustic guitar, jazz bass, and the shimmering orchestral strings.

- **Action 2:** The Baroque Texture: Pay attention to the strings (often viola and cello). They do not provide grand washes of sound; rather, they play precise, elegant counter-melodies and arpeggios that lend the music the texture and intimacy of a Baroque chamber consort, reflecting the delicate sound of the viola da gamba discussed in Chapter 5.

Deeper Dive: The Timeless Narrative

Morrison successfully demonstrated that the power of Celtic melody, when freed from pop structure, could create a timeless, profound narrative that transcended genre, echoing O'Carolan's success at blending native tunes with formal, classical arrangements centuries earlier.

THE UNIFIED GROUND

Conclusion: The Unified Soundscape: The Continuum of UK Music

We began this journey by examining two seemingly disparate traditions: the formal, often complex grief of the Baroque court and the simple, unadorned truth of the Folk fields. But by listening closely — tracing bass lines, monitoring the function of drones, and following the voices — we find they do not exist in separate worlds; rather, they profoundly inform one another at their deepest structural level.

Resonance, Not Rupture

The consistency of techniques across three centuries reveals that musical repetition isn't coincidence — it's cultural DNA.

The Power of Repetition: The simple, repeating motif, whether a four-chord structure or a continuous note, served as the indispensable backbone for both traditions. This fundamental stability allows for emotional and narrative expansion. We hear it in the ground bass of Purcell's Dido's Lament, in the endlessly variable La Folia progression that Marin Marais transformed, and in the unchanging, low drone of the Copper Family's a cappella harmonies. From Purcell's chromatics to the Coppers' harmonies, the ground provides the anchor.

The Economy of Intimacy: Both Baroque chamber music and the folk club prioritize intimacy over scale. The delicate, fretted texture of the viola da gamba and the intricate counterpoint of Jansch and Renbourn mirrors the private, unamplified setting of the a cappella fields. This chamber economy forces the performer to focus power into clarity and emotional precision, proving that narrative strength requires only essential resources, whether sung in a Rottingdean pub or played in a 17th-century drawing room.

Melodies Endure: The core melodies and simple dance rhythms preserved in Playford's Dancing Master are the same essential patterns that O'Carolan formalized in the 18th century, and that Blowzabella electrifies today. The melodies endure, varied by ornamentation and arrangement, yet fundamentally pure.

This "**Listening Guide**" is, therefore, an invitation to listen not for difference, but for resonance. The soundscape of early and modern UK music is not a fracture but a unified field, where the sophisticated ornament of the court and the simple story of the downs are two sides of the same coin: human expression. In an age of algorithms and playlists, this fusion reminds us that music is a continuum—intimate, historical, and perpetually alive.

Recommendations for Deeper Listening

To continue your journey tracing these lines of influence and fusion, seek out these complementary artists who further explore the sonic landscape of UK Baroque and Folk:

Ensemble Focus (Baroque/Early Music)
The work of **Jordi Savall** and **Hespèrion XX/XXI** (especially their 2005 Altre Follie), for their deep, soulful engagement with the viola da gamba tradition and the Folias variations. Savall's gamba weaves textures like a master storyteller's voice, bridging Marais to Iberian folk roots.

Solo Folk Ingenuity (Modern Revival)
Richard Thompson (especially his 1972 debut Henry the Human Fly), for a songwriting style deeply informed by the structure and melancholy of traditional English ballads. Tracks like *"Shaky Nancy"* echo ballad narratives with guitar ostinatos akin to Baroque ground basses. Thompson's wry despair channels Purcell's restraint.

Modern Fusion (Classical & Folk)
The choral arrangements of composer **John Rutter** (e.g., 1979's Five Traditional Songs featuring "O Waly, Waly"), demonstrating the ongoing, seamless dialogue between traditional melodies and structured, classically-informed compositions. Rutter's choral bloom fuses Playford's dances with Baroque poise.

Bonus: Raucous Revival
The Carnival Band with Maddy Prior (Sing Lustily and with Good Cheer, 1990) for raucous, period-instrument revivals of carols and dances. Their pipes and voices evoke Blowzabella's powerful, drone-based energy but in the raucous, communal form of Playford's music.

www.ingramcontent.com/pod-product-compliance
Lightning Source LLC
Chambersburg PA
CBHW020811130626
46554CB00006B/2376